M000034891

For Dear Life

Gail,
thank you for sharing your
poetry wisdom. One of my
best decisions was joining the
BHPC. So many great moments.

poems by

Jessica Dubey

Jessica Dubey

Finishing Line Press
Georgetown, Kentucky

For Dear Life

ACKNOWLEDGMENTS

Many thanks to the publications in which the following poems originally
appeared.

"My Husband Tries to Record the Sound in His Ear," *Barren Magazine*
"Entering the ICU," *Gulf Stream Literary Magazine*
"Rewired," *North of Oxford*
"They Don't Shave Your Head Anymore," *Rat's Ass Review*
"Two Years after Brain Surgery I Contemplate My Husband's Former Self,"
American Poetry Journal

Publisher: Leah Huete de Maines
Editor: Christen Kincaid
Cover Art: Jessica Dubey
Author Photo: Emily Bond, Emmy Marie Photography
Cover Design: Elizabeth Maines McCleavy

Order online: www.finishinglinepress.com
also available on amazon.com

Author inquiries and mail orders:
Finishing Line Press
PO Box 1626
Georgetown, Kentucky 40324
USA

Table of Contents

*DEDICATED with love to my husband, Neil,
the strongest man I know
And to
E. Sander Connolly, Jr., MD; Sean D. Lavine, MD;
Evangeline Reyes-Pastorella, FNP-C; and the physicians, nurses,
and staff of Columbia Presbyterian Hospital Neuro ICU
for their exceptional care and compassion*

*I'd also like to express my gratitude for my local writing group,
The Grapevine Poets, who have taught me the importance and joy
of being part of a poetry community. To Gail DiMaggio and all of
the Boiler House Poets Collective who are simply brilliant and,
though I see them only once a year, feel like family. To Elizabeth
Cohen for her insight and spot-on advice. To Andrei Guruianu
whose workshops early in my writing journey inspired and
motivated me. To Connie Kallechey Barnes who has been
in my corner since the beginning. And to Neil and our children,
Ashton and Anya, for their love and support.*

.

"Grief and resilience live together."
— *Michelle Obama,* Becoming

My Husband Tries to Record the Sound in His Ear

I picked up a shell on the beach
it held   the ocean
When he turned to me at night
I heard the same wave
crashing in his ear
He said   it sounded like madness
begged me to draw it out
It takes a special kind of talent
I told him   to siphon the seas
from the body of one man
I asked him   how long
had the water flowed through him
He said   he was a mountain
when it started
now he's a grain of sand

Entering the ICU

The air tastes of
something that
lock onto my skin
They resist
I want to live
Now I stand
A set of doors
I pull
I imagine
hand sanitizer
across the moat
A man in his room
around my husband
back
then spreads it

spoiled milk
was safe to drink
follow me back to my hotel
hot showers and rainstorms
the imperfection
at the entrance
and a sign stand
at the dispenser
filling my cupped hands
to anoint him
that surrounds his brain
pushes a mop
makes a dirty outline
into the bucket
& all its misery

a day ago
Its molecules
climb into bed with me
I want to crawl away
of the past
of the ICU
between us
this mindless new ritual
an offering
to seep into his pores
to destroy the darkness
traces the floor
dips the disheveled head
of wretched water
to the next room

Ten Days

He says he wants to remember
 My face at first light
Brilliant as a fluorescent sun
 He says he wants to remember
Breath spilling back into his chest
 The warm touch
Of my always-cold hands
 The familiar hum of words
Me saying, "Squeeze my hand"
 He says he wants to remember
The view from his 8th floor tower
 The terraced park below
He says he wants to remember
 The taste of awakening
My lips on his
 Just the two of us
He says he wants to remember
 When he first opened his eyes
He says he wants to remember

He doesn't remember
 Our children arranged in the room
Their cloud of emotion
 He doesn't remember
His shipwrecked body
 Shuddering against the anesthesia
Through the cold depths
 Dragged to the surface fentanyl-free
The surgeon saying, "Squeeze my hand"
 He doesn't remember
His brain remaking itself
 Skull knitting & clicking into place
He doesn't remember
 His lips locked in a long kiss
With the breathing tube
 Just him and his pain
He doesn't remember
 His silent picture eyes
He doesn't remember

When did you first notice symptoms?

57 y.o. male with worsening headaches, possible surgical intervention. Will start with diagnostic angio and discuss options with patient **Why are we interrogating the body** and family. 57 y.o. male with **as if it were the great betrayer?** worsening headaches, possible **Wasn't it the body** surgical intervention. Will start with **that rebelled against the silence** diagnostic angio and discuss options **and shook us until we noticed?** with patient and family. 57 y.o. male with worsening headaches, possible surgical intervention. Will start with diagnostic angio and discuss options with patient and family.

In that other reality

I am alone   Alone

His brain swells   the whole of him

            irretrievable

I throw away

         pack away

               give away

years 1 through 33

I try to turn that last year around   It is still 33

It resists all attempts at 34

I bake a cake for the next anniversary

      It doesn't come

I try to mix up the collated years

put number three   last

           move 33 to the middle

The years bite back

Retrograde

We are never out of the woods
in this monotonous landscape,
shoulder to shoulder
with old-growth trees.
No room to dodge falling fruit
or small mishaps with outsized consequences.
He slips on the ice.
The spongy spot at the back of his skull
eight months earlier
ceremoniously opened
in the OR of New York Presbyterian.
That is where he lands.
His head takes the full impact
of the frozen ground
like the head of a crash dummy.
But not in slow motion.
No freezeframe.
No slamming it all into reverse,
his body levitating horizontal to the ground,
then upright, walking it backwards
through the door.
Then at 2x speed, 3x speed. Back, back,
back before it all went wrong. Before
those delicate little branches in his head
made bad connections,
forcing the blood to flow in retrograde.
Forcing us back into the woods.

Elegy for the Future

There are footsteps in the snow
    with no end
        no beginning
I know
    I followed them   I had a plan

That's the setup
    and the punch line
        Autocorrect

we   had a plan   Now
we plan for another
        future
that may not include   a future

I just ordered new luggage   We
are on a plane
    that only taxis   no liftoff

no peanuts   no leg room   no emergency escape

I used to use cocktail napkins
    as blueprints
        for poems
    I'd never   write

    Matchbooks
were too small   too incendiary

          I want
to collect tiny soaps   shampoo bottles
          those Barbie-sized sewing kits   That

should be my children's inheritance   Not
this   elegy
I'm scrawling

on a tray table   pretending
          I'm still in flight

Eclipse

In our two-dollar glasses
we are uncompassed.
All reverence for calendars
and clocks is lost.

We know the sun will leave us.
We know it will return.
It's the only thing we know.
And even that's not certain

as anesthesia lulls his brain to sleep.
Constellations disappear.
There are no stars
in his primitive night.

Then the moon peels back
like an eyelid.

As If in Prayer

He saved spit in his mouth,
day after day collected thimblefuls
in his cheeks
until there was enough to swish
then swallowed hard.
All this in defiance of doctor's orders:
Nothing by mouth.
What they couldn't see
they couldn't stop.
It was his game to play,
the psychosis of the ICU
a dice game rattling around
in his head.
Instead of sleep he obsessed
about ice chips
and long draws from a straw.
His bed just feet from the sink,
he fantasized standing on its lip
hands pressed together
before he dove in.

The Dog Doesn't Eat

I add meat to his dog food. A few bites,
then he turns away from it.
For a while he likes scallops.
We run out of enticement.
I don't know it yet, but he'll be gone
in a matter of days.

A few weeks later my husband
teeters on the same edge.
The surgeon removes
the breathing tube,
forbids food and water.

So I don't eat,
except in my hotel room at night,
cookie crumbs making the hotel sheets itchier.
I leave his hospital room
to steal sips of water.
IV drips through battered veins.

The night nurses are told
not to give in to his demands
for ice chips.
He grabs my arm, squeezes too tight.
We get smaller together,
each day a little more shrunken.

The day he passes his swallow test, I run
to the ice machine, fill a cup for him.
I'm so happy to be the one
to give him what he wants.
I set it before him. He turns away.
He says the doctors are killing him.
I am killing him.

When to Call Your Doctor

When an artery and a vein make abnormal connections
When vein artery diagnose unnatural tension
When results may blockage jumble
When return later life struggle
Onset is hemorrhage route
Headache vomit sudden bout
Origin flow foggy causation
Fistula location, location
Vision issues prognosis theory
Unusual may occur worry

Day Six

"Small progress is still progress."
Anonymous

Two nurses, identical.
Two carts, two mop buckets.
Two doors.

How many fingers am I holding up?
The doctor flashes a peace sign.

Four, he answers.
Same test the next day, same answer.

Then the same test, different question.
How many of your wife do you see?

Today he smiles.
Two. I see two of her.

Swallow This

The scope is fed to the nose
which swallows it whole.
Its eye opens on its soft, wet
surroundings. Searches
for the pink flap that flies open
and shut like an unlatched door
in a summer storm.
Everything that enters
the mouth is dyed
to look like Easter grass.
Applesauce, ice chips, milk
in order—thick, thinner, thinnest.
The milk rushes in
like the tide, then washes out,
some pooling around the opening,
threatening to spill over.
This happens in real time.
The potential for disaster
hanging on a droplet
that wants so badly to misbehave,
to slide down the airway,
to make silent chaos.

Rewired

This is not how I envisioned my day—
drenched in humidity, hand extended
to receive screws and bolts,
brackets and washers.
My husband leans over an engine
four weeks after surgery,
four weeks after his head was pried open
like the hood of this car
so the surgeon could reach in,
remove a piece of his skull, cauterize
and staple him back together.
I cringe each time he straightens up,
hits his head on the hood,
imagine him in one of the helmets
designed for infants whose heads
are misshapen at birth.
All of his reshaping unseen,
neuroplasticity reconnecting
spark plug wires and intake hoses
so that his brain recognizes
the horizon rather than being adrift.
I know he should rest, but
maybe this is what he needs most,
to use his hands and his head
bent over an engine.
Instead of the incessant hum in his ear,
he hears his father's voice
instructing him
how to dismantle a machine,
then make it work again.

They Don't Shave Your Head Anymore

I want to reach out and touch the bald head
of the man sitting in front of me, forbidden
as a museum painting,
like the photorealist's rendition
of fruit and cheese I saw at a gallery
the night before.
I held myself back wanting to pluck
one of the glistening grapes
and pop it in my mouth—that kind
of temptation—to run my hand
over the smooth scape
of his head, scarless
unless you count the ring of freckles
the sun left behind, those ripe little spots
on an otherwise untouched scalp.

I think about the sickle-shaped scar
on my husband's head, now buried
under a healthy crop of hair.
How even after it healed
he didn't want me to touch it.
How I longed to run my fingers
through his hair the way I did
on road trips, my left hand
slipping past his shoulder,
my fingers raking the soft locks,
massaging his scalp as he drove.

They don't shave your head anymore
before the scalpel makes that decisive cut.
Radiation had already taken so much
of his hair. What was left
laid down on either side of the incision,
the skin held closed by a long track
of tightly-spaced staples
from the nape to the peak of his head,
the most badass thing I'd ever seen.
I took a picture so he could see it later,
after the pain had gained some distance.

He wondered for months
if his hair would grow back.
Now that it has, he tells his barber
to cut it short, really short,
so he doesn't have to comb it anymore,
so every morning
he just has to run his fingers through it.

Two Years After Brain Surgery
I Contemplate My Husband's Former Self

After the sculpture, Daddy in the Dark, by John Chamberlain

We watch as a crane picks apart a car.
    It reaches in to pull the engine, a vulture
        going straight for the belly.

It drops the block onto a pile then turns back
    for the carcass, wraps its claw around it,
        lets it fall into the crusher

like a used napkin. Its body implodes
    right before our eyes.
        We have been watching this video

for half an hour. I sit on a stool next to his chair,
    notice his fingers coaxing an imaginary controller.
        I take his other hand

as a white sedan leaves the crusher, a ghost of a car,
    like the one we saw mangled into art,
        all the unnatural joints

welded to keep it intact and upright, a bruised heart
    nestled in its chromium-plated wreckage,
        like a transformer

gone horribly wrong—a car that wants to turn itself
    into a rocket ship or a wind chime
        frozen mid-transformation.

I tell him I can't watch anymore. He hits pause as one more
    car dangles above the machinery about to be remade
        into something not quite itself.

Does the calm love the storm?

We bicker. There was a time
it seemed cruel to hope
for petty squabbles.
He leaves every light on
as if lighting a landing strip.
I flip the switches, complain
about the utility bill.
He feeds the dog sugary cereal,
scattering it like pigeon feed
on the kitchen floor.
I shoo the dog,
scold him for the mess.
We have settled back into
comfort, but even that
is disquieting at times.
I wonder if I'm floating
on an ocean letting
the salt's sting cleanse the wound
of last year.
Or have I allowed myself
to float so far out
I no longer see the shore?

For Dear Life

"Everything I've ever let go of has claw marks on it."
David Foster Wallace

After months of rehab
        through recovery's uncertain re-entry

He comes back from a point
        so far away it seems like gone

We resettle what was shaken
        pick up where we left off living

Now, of all times, I go through boxes
        that moved with us twice

Take the box-cutter
        slice them open like overripe fruit

Try to understand
        the significance of holding on

Reassign meaning, keep nothing
        hold onto everything

Jessica **Dubey's** poetry flows from her experiences as a life-long resident of upstate New York. She is a member of the Boiler House Poets Collective which convenes annually for a poetry residency at The Studios of the Massachusetts Museum of Contemporary Art. Jessica has been nominated for a Best of the Net and was Kissing Dynamite's September 2019 featured poet. She is a graduate of Syracuse University's S.I. Newhouse School of Public Communications and worked as a magazine editor, a marketing manager in the healthcare field, and later a freelance writer. Her poetry has appeared in numerous journals including *Oxidant | Engine, Barren Magazine, Gulf Stream Literary Magazine, North of Oxford,* and *The American Journal of Poetry. For Dear Life* is her first chapbook.

CPSIA information can be obtained
at www.ICGtesting.com
Printed in the USA
BVHW041021070522
636391BV00002B/114